MYSTERIES OF HISTORY

THE MYSTERY OF THE NAZCA LINES

by Bonnie Hinman

Content Consultant
Michael Malpass, PhD
Professor of Anthropology
Ithaca College

abdopublishing.com

Published by Abdo Publishing, a division of ABDO, PO Box 398166, Minneapolis, Minnesota 55439. Copyright © 2016 by Abdo Consulting Group, Inc. International copyrights reserved in all countries. No part of this book may be reproduced in any form without written permission from the publisher. Core Library™ is a trademark and logo of Abdo Publishing.

Printed in the United States of America, North Mankato, Minnesota
082015
012016

Cover Photo: Shutterstock Images
Interior Photos: Shutterstock Images, 1; Eduardo Herran/EPA/Newscom, 4; Henry L. Batterman Fund, 7; Alejandro Balaguer/AP Images, 10; iStockphoto, 13, 43; Alexander Pöschel/ ImageBroker/Newscom, 15; Mike Theiss/National Geographic Creative/Corbis, 18; Ingram Publishing/Newscom, 21, 32; Bettmann/Corbis, 24; Daniel Thory/REX/Newscom, 26; El Comercio/AP Images, 31, 45; US/Japan ASTER Science Team/JAROS/ERSDAC/MITI/GSFC/ NASA, 34; Red Line Editorial, 37; Kyodo/AP Images, 40

Editor: Mirella Miller
Series Designer: Ryan Gale

Library of Congress Control Number: 2015945992

Cataloging-in-Publication Data
Hinman, Bonnie.
  The mystery of the Nazca Lines / Bonnie Hinman.
   p. cm. -- (Mysteries of history)
ISBN 978-1-68078-025-3 (lib. bdg.)
Includes bibliographical references and index.
1. Nazca Lines Site (Peru)--Juvenile literature. 2. Indians of South America--Peru--Juvenile literature.   I. Title.
985--dc23

2015945992

CONTENTS

CHAPTER ONE
Lines on the Pampa 4

CHAPTER TWO
Protector of the Lines 10

CHAPTER THREE
Computers, Aliens, and Balloons 18

CHAPTER FOUR
Practical Theories 26

CHAPTER FIVE
The Search Goes On 34

Weighing the Evidence 42

Stop and Think 44

Glossary 46

Learn More 47

Index 48

About the Author 48

CHAPTER ONE

LINES ON THE PAMPA

In 1927 Peruvian archaeologist Toribio Mejia Xesspe hiked into a high dune near his dig site to take a look at the pampa, or plateau, below. He was working on a burial dig site in southern Peru near the ruins of the ancient city of Cahuachi. As Mejia scanned the desert below, he saw something strange. Light-colored lines on the darker-colored desert floor stretched into the distance as straight as rulers. Were

An aerial view of the dog geoglyph in southern Peru

they a natural feature? How could that happen? If not natural, how and why would people create them? The mystery of the Nazca Lines began that day.

The Nazca Lines are geoglyphs, or ground drawings. The name comes from the hundreds of straight lines that crisscross the pampa between two river valleys. Almost all of the geoglyphs are in an area of 310 square miles (803 sq km). There are drawings of animals, plants, and a few human shapes. Geometric figures such as rectangles, trapezoids, and spirals can also be seen. The huge drawings are clearest when viewed from an airplane but can also be seen from hills and other high places.

Nazca Culture

Archaeologists believe the Nazca made the geoglyphs from approximately 100 BCE to 650 CE. The Nazca lived in narrow river valleys along the southern Peruvian coast on the west side of the Andes Mountains. The climate was hot and dry since rain almost never fell on the desert. Water came from the

The Nazca potters used at least 12 different colors.

rivers that flowed from the Andes Mountains to the Pacific Ocean.

The Nazca did not have a central government. They lived in many small villages led by chiefs. They shared a common religion and culture and are famous for the colorful and detailed pottery they produced. However, the Nazca Lines are the most well known creations of the Nazca. The Nazca did not have a

PERSPECTIVES
Which Came First?

Archaeologist Persis Clarkson dated pottery remains found near the geoglyphs largely between 200 and 600 CE but believed some were made as late as 1000 CE. This would mean another culture made some of the geoglyphs, since evidence suggests the Nazca disappeared before 1000 CE. However, archaeologist Helaine Silverman disagrees. She believes all of the Nazca Lines were made between 200 and 600 CE. She thinks the Nazca made all of the geoglyphs.

written language and left no record of why they built the geoglyphs on the sandy pampa.

The Mystery of the Lines

The mystery of the Nazca Lines has never been about how they were made. Archaeologists know from research that the Nazca scraped away the top dark layer of desert varnish to reveal the white layer underneath. The Nazca combined lines of different widths and lengths to make the drawings. The lines and geometrical figures were created using some sort of measurement unit.

Scientists are not sure what the unit was, but it allowed the Nazca to make very straight lines.

Mejia was the first modern scientist to discover the Nazca Lines, but he was not the last to investigate the geoglyphs in the desert of Peru. Many questions remain. Scientists may know how the lines were made, but they do not know how the people designed the figures and shapes. How were the designs transferred onto the desert ground? And by far the biggest mystery, why were the lines made? Scientists and archaeologists have spent almost 100 years trying to answer these questions.

Desert Varnish

Desert varnish is a paper-thin, dark coating that appears on rocks in desert areas. The rocks around the Nazca Lines are covered with desert varnish. It can take thousands of years for the coating to become dark enough to see. The coating is made of manganese and clay. Morning dew helps cement the varnish to the rocks, but rain washes it away.

CHAPTER TWO

PROTECTOR OF THE LINES

No person has been more important to the Nazca Lines mystery than Maria Reiche. She was a mathematician who spent more than 50 years investigating the mysterious lines in Peru. Reiche left her home in Germany in 1932. Dictator Adolf Hitler had begun his rise to power, and Reiche wanted to escape the political unrest. She remained in Peru for the majority of her life and eventually became

Reiche also worked as a teacher and translator while living in Peru.

Other Geoglyphs

The Nazca Lines are the most famous geoglyphs, but they are not the only ones in the world. The Paracas Candelabra is also in Peru, and the Atacama Giant is in nearby Chile. England, Saudi Arabia, Australia, and the United States also have geoglyphs with different styles and from different eras. A geoglyph of an elk or moose found in Russia may be the oldest geoglyph discovered. Tools found near it date from 4000 to 3000 BCE.

a Peruvian citizen. She met Mejia, who took her on her first trip to see the Nazca Lines. Reiche later wrote that this trip put a spell on her.

Paul Kosok

Reiche met Paul Kosok when she did a translation job for him in 1941. He was in Peru studying ancient irrigation systems. When Kosok heard of the Nazca Lines, he immediately thought they were irrigation ditches.

A trip to the desert changed his mind. By chance, Kosok's wife Rose took a picture of him among the lines at sunset in June 1941. The sun was setting almost exactly at the end of one of the Nazca Lines.

Kosok needed Reiche to do more research on his astronomy map theory.

Kosok later said he and his wife thought they had happened upon the world's largest astronomy book.

Kosok could not stay in Peru to investigate his theory. He knew Reiche had seen the Nazca Lines and asked her to take on the project. She agreed and visited the lines again in December 1941. World War II (1939–1945) kept Reiche from researching immediately. She did what she could but was not

PERSPECTIVES
Ruler of the Pampa

Almost all modern archaeologists honor Reiche as the dedicated preserver of the Nazca Lines. However, some scientists thought her determination to prove the astronomical theory was too narrow. She had Professor Anthony Aveni arrested for trespassing when he used a balloon to take low-level pictures of the lines. Aveni believed Reiche saw his different ideas as a threat. The Peruvian government and the local citizens allowed Reiche free rein over the lines, and she did not welcome anyone she had not chosen to view the lines. Reiche stuck to her theory, while Aveni and many other researchers disagreed. This difference led to many clashes in Reiche's later years.

able to live full time near the Nazca Lines until the late 1940s. After that, measuring, photographing, and protecting the Nazca Lines consumed the rest of her life. Reiche agreed with Kosok that the geoglyphs were some type of astronomical calendar. The pair believed the Nazca needed a calendar to know when to expect rain to arrive each year.

Reiche believed the straight lines would point to a star at one time but be out of line with that star 100 years later. This

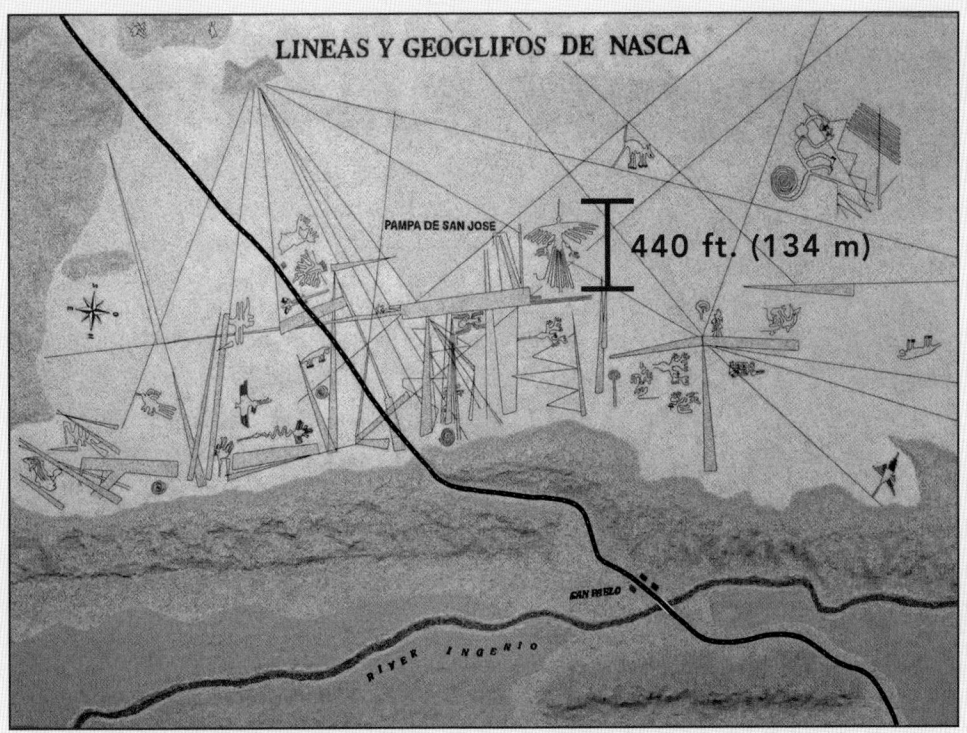

Nazca Lines Map
The area in which the Nazca Lines are located is relatively small compared to the size of Peru and the size of South America. Even so, the figures and lines are huge. The condor drawing is approximately 440 feet (134 m) long. Does the diagram help you understand what you might see if you flew in an airplane over the Nazca Valley?

was a possible explanation for all of the parallel lines. The Nazca simply built a new line when the old one no longer pointed directly at the star.

Guarding the Lines

Reiche convinced the Peruvian Air Force to take aerial photos of the lines and figures between 1944 and 1947. Many of the local people thought Reiche was crazy. She spent months on the hot desert ground taking pictures and sweeping debris from the geoglyphs. The Peruvian people changed their minds about Reiche when they saw she only wanted to protect the mysterious lines. Reiche used the funds from the sale of her first book, *Mystery on the Desert*, to pay guards to protect the lines from tourists who hiked over them.

Many other theories about the Nazca Lines were published during the years Reiche spent doing her own research. She never wavered from her own theory of the lines being an astronomical calendar. The biggest challenge to Reiche and Kosok's theory came in 1968 from a computer.

STRAIGHT TO THE SOURCE

Maria Reiche explains how the Nazca Lines were made in this excerpt from her 1949 book, *Mystery on the Desert*:

> As we follow the gigantic designs on the ground, using as roadmaps the vertical aerial photographs, we see that they are very shallow surface depressions. Their light color has been produced by a very simple process.
>
> A reddish brown, almost black, color characterizes the plains and mountains of this region, which is exceptionally rich in iron. Being produced by oxidation and the effect of thousands of years of daily morning dew followed by excessive heat, this color does not reach deeper than one or two inches. The stones and gravel underneath are yellowish white.
>
> This contrast made it possible to use the level surfaces as immense blackboards on which white designs could be produced on a dark background by simply removing the upper layer of black stones.
>
> Source: Maria Reiche. Mystery on the Desert. Lima, Peru: 1949. Print. 2.

Back It Up

Reiche has used evidence to support the point she wishes to make. Write a paragraph describing the point the author is making. Then write down two kinds of evidence she used to make her point.

CHAPTER THREE

COMPUTERS, ALIENS, AND BALLOONS

Astronomer Gerald Hawkins was already well known among scientists when he began a study of the Nazca Lines in 1967. He had proposed a debated theory about Stonehenge in England, which he first wrote about in 1963. Using a computer, Hawkins believed he proved the huge standing rocks were both an observatory and a calendar for ancient residents of southern England.

Other than Kosok and Reiche's theory, many other scientists and researchers came up with their own ideas about the Nazca Lines.

Archaeologists greeted Hawkins's conclusions about Stonehenge with great disbelief.

Hawkins planned to use the same techniques to prove whether or not the Nazca Lines were an astronomical calendar. Hawkins and his team of assistants surveyed the lines on the ground and used aerial photographs to gather more data. After the study was completed in December 1968, Hawkins fed the information into a computer.

When Hawkins looked at the computer's results, he saw that some of the lines pointed to certain stars. These were probably chance alignments, as the great majority of the lines do not point to any stars or other celestial objects. He

Cahuachi

The ruins of the ancient city of Cahuachi are located on the south bank of the Nazca River near the Nazca Lines. Some of the lines point directly at Cahuachi. At first archaeologists believed Cahuachi was the capital city of the Nazca. Now they think it was a city with no permanent residents.

The Cahuachi ceremonial center has dozens of adobe pyramids built into the desert sands, some of which overlook the Nazca Lines.

concluded the Nazca Lines were not an astronomical calendar.

Other scientists, including Anthony Aveni, believed Hawkins's study samples were too small and ignored known facts about the Southern Hemisphere's night sky. Above all, Aveni did not think there was one explanation for the Nazca Lines, particularly a single mathematical explanation. Whether or not Hawkins was correct, his computer work and results opened the door for new theories about the Nazca Lines.

Aliens

One of the most famous theories about the Nazca Lines was published in the book *Chariots of the Gods* in 1968. Author Erich von Däniken proposed the lines might have been airfields for outer space visitors. The Nazca Lines were only one of the ancient mysteries included in von Däniken's book, but the airfield theory quickly became well known and popular.

The 1970s were a time when people were more interested in aliens than ever before. Special effects in movies made it seem possible there was life beyond Earth. Von Däniken's theory caught the public's attention.

Balloons

Explorer Jim Woodman not only had a different theory, but also did his best to prove it in a practical way. Woodman was convinced the Nazca had soared over the desert in hot-air balloons to look at their drawings while worshipping the sun.

Woodman built a hot-air balloon to fly over the pampa. He used materials he thought would have been available to the Nazca. Woven reeds made up the basket, while tightly woven cotton fabric formed the triangular balloon walls. Body bags found in ancient cemeteries had similar woven fabrics. Reed cords held everything together. Only later did archaeologists point out that the reeds did not grow in the desert. They grew approximately 395 miles

PERSPECTIVES
Priests vs. Shamans

Archaeologist Kosok believed a priestly class ruled the Nazca. He said priests used an astronomical calendar to predict water flow, which would determine planting times. This ability gave the priests enormous power over their people. Archaeologists Helaine Silverman and Donald A. Proulx say instead that shamans guided the Nazca's religious practices. They define priests as being full-time experts who preside over temples and shrines. Among the Nazca, community members became part-time shamans who communicated between the spirit world and the everyday world.

Woodman and many other researchers have taken to the sky to try to solve the mystery surrounding the Nazca Lines.

(636 km) away from the Nazca Lines. It took four hours to fill the balloon with hot air from a huge fire. The balloon flew for a short time with little control from its pilot. Although it was a short flight, Woodman stuck by his theory.

Ancient aliens and balloonists may sound unlikely, but other strange theories existed in the years following the 1927 Nazca Lines discovery. Memorials, giant looms, and running tracks popped up as proposed answers to the mystery of the Nazca Lines.

STRAIGHT TO THE SOURCE

In the excerpt below, author Erich von Däniken explains his theory about the purpose of the Nazca Lines:

> Seen from the air, the clear-cut impression that the 37-mile-long [60 km] plain of Nazca made on me was that of an airfield! What is so farfetched about the idea? What purpose did the lines at Nazca serve? It is not yet possible to say with certainty whether the plain of Nazca was ever an airfield. What is wrong with the idea that the lines were laid out to say to the "gods": "Land here! Everything has been prepared as you ordered." The builders of the geometrical figures may have had no idea what they were doing. But perhaps they knew perfectly well what the "gods" needed in order to land.
>
> Source: Erich von Däniken. Chariots of the Gods: Unsolved Mysteries of the Past. New York: Berkley, 1999. Print. 33.

Back It Up

Von Däniken is using evidence to support a point. Write a paragraph describing the point the author is making. Then write down two or three pieces of evidence von Däniken does or does not have to make his point.

CHAPTER FOUR

PRACTICAL THEORIES

The mystery of the Nazca Lines has always been wide open to theories. Many of the men and women who proposed these theories concentrated on finding a practical purpose for the Nazca Lines. They thought the Nazca must have had good reason for building the huge drawings and lines. Many people believe this reason was for something other than rituals or artistic creation.

Many of the Nazca Lines are on high ridges, which means they were likely not used for farming.

Rossel Castro was a Peruvian priest and an archaeologist in the 1940s. He believed the large cleared areas of the Nazca Lines were former fields farmed by the Nazca. Castro stated the raised edges of the clearings would help hold moisture. The inside of the lines could be piled high with natural fertilizer, such as seaweed and llama dung. The biggest problem with this theory is that most of the clearings made by the Nazca Lines are on high ridges. How would farmers have transported water from below up to their fields? And why would they do this if plenty of farmland was in nearby river valleys?

Swiss professor and author Henri Stierlin wrote in 1983 that the clearings were giant fabric workshops. He believed that miles-long cotton threads were laid out in the clearings and then woven into huge pieces of cloth. Stierlin proposed that many people formed a human loom, using the lines as guides. Unusually long burial cloths have been found wrapped around bodies in ancient cemeteries located near villages along the Peruvian coast. Archaeologists believe extremely long pieces of cloth could have been made with special looms. There is no evidence, however, to support Stierlin's theory about the Nazca Lines being a loom.

Olympic Games and Memorials

German engineer George von Breunig came up with an equally interesting theory in 1980. After seeing the figures in Peru, von Breunig speculated the Nazca Lines were running tracks. He believed there

PERSPECTIVES
Munck's Theory

Carl Munck is a self-described studier of ancient codes. Munck says ancient sites, including the Nazca Lines, contain codes showing their position on Earth. He believes the geometric angles of the Nazca Lines describe their position on Earth similar to a map. Munck's theory requires that the Nazca understood and used complex math. Munck gave a radio interview in 2012 that undermined his credibility. In the interview he described how aliens took him up in a spaceship over the Nazca Lines in 1982. He said the aliens taught him their form of math, which he is using to crack codes.

> ## El Niño
>
> A climate pattern called El Niño hits Peru every two to seven years. The pattern varies in strength, but a very strong pattern could affect the Nazca Lines. El Niño happens when there is an unusual warming of surface waters along the west coast of South America. This warming affects ocean temperatures, currents, fishing, and local weather from Australia to South America. The heavy rain a strong El Niño may bring to the Peruvian desert could alter or even destroy the geoglyphs.

might have been some sort of Nazca athletic competitions, similar to the Olympic Games. Von Breunig found some historical references to runners during the Inca time, which was many years after the Nazca lived. Von Breunig also said the paths were piled at the curves, similar to a running track. Few people other than von Breunig himself were convinced the ancient Nazca hosted their own Olympic games.

Australian Robert Bast moved away from practical theories. In 2006 he proposed the drawings of animals and humans, which appear to be lying on the

In 1998 mudslides from El Niño damaged some of the Nazca Lines.

31

Most scientists do not agree with Bast's theory of the geoglyphs being a great flood memorial.

ground, were memorials to a great flood. This flood left behind dead humans and animals as represented by the figures in the desert. Many cultures around the world have a flood myth. These cultures pass on stories of a great flood that passed over Earth thousands of years ago. There is, however, no proof the Nazca Lines had anything to do with a flood myth. Eventually archaeologists and other scientists returned to theories proposed early in the search for the Nazca Lines' purpose. These theories were both practical and religious.

FURTHER EVIDENCE

Chapter Four presents several theories about the purpose of the Nazca Lines. What is the main point of the chapter? The website below gives more information not present in Chapter Four. Find three facts in the article that are not mentioned in Chapter Four. Do these facts support an existing piece of evidence in the chapter? Or do they offer a new piece of evidence?

The Sacred Landscape
mycorelibrary.com/nazca-lines

CHAPTER FIVE

THE SEARCH GOES ON

In recent years, new theories about the purpose of the Nazca Lines have begun to sound more believable. Water is a big part of new Nazca Lines theories. Water was the most important aspect of Nazca life. They lived successfully in the desert for hundreds of years. Having enough water was a daily task. The theory that the Nazca Lines were maps of underground water sources seems reasonable.

With more modern technology becoming available, scientists and researchers can use things such as satellite images to try to better understand the Nazca Lines.

Independent scholar David Johnson was the first researcher to spend several years in the field trying to prove the water map theory. He reported that aquifers, or underground water sources, happen most often when two or more geological faults cross each other. A fault appears when rock layers in Earth's crust fracture and move past each other on either side of the break. Some of the geometric geoglyphs mark these faults and show where the water flows underground from the mountains.

Johnson said the zigzag lines marked areas where there was no underground water. Figures marked where aquifers changed directions. While interested in Johnson's theory, other scientists believe Johnson did not use proper scientific methods in his study. They want more research done.

Return to Mejia's Theory

Mejia's original theory about the lines said they were ritual pathways, an idea to which archaeologists have returned. He believed the Nazca may have walked the

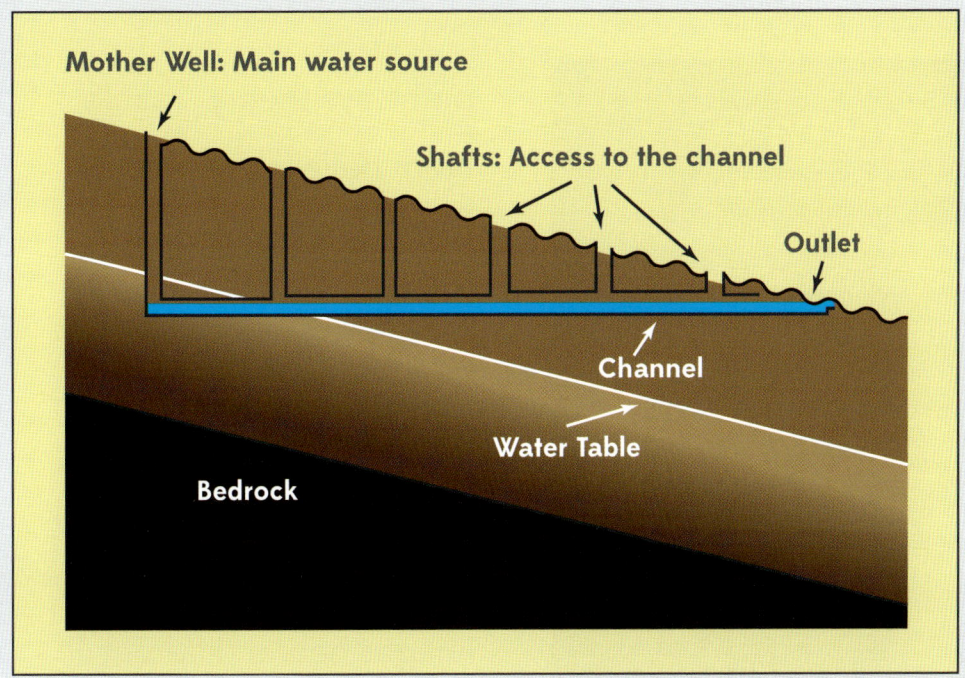

Puquios

Puquios are ancient wells developed to tap underground water sources in the Nazca region. Many scientists believe the Nazca built the puquios, while others think they were built later. Puquios are still used today in Peru. This diagram shows a cross section of a puquio. Do you think the Nazca could have built puquios with the materials and tools they had?

pathways to worship the water gods. This ties into the Nazca's need for sufficient water supplies.

Yamagata University of Japan opened a research center in Nazca in 2012. Professor Masato Sakai, leader of the research team, presented new findings in April 2015. These findings support the ritual

> **New Geoglyphs**
>
> A Peruvian pilot spotted new geoglyphs on hills near the El Ingenio Valley in July 2014. He believes sandstorms blew away soil that had covered them for as many as 2,000 years. The new figures included a snake, a bird, and a llama. New zigzag lines appeared as well.

pathways theory. Sakai's team believes there were two groups of people building the Nazca Lines. One group built animal geoglyphs that clustered along a route to Cahuachi. Another group built images near a different route to Cahuachi. Both groups walked the Nazca Lines as they took offerings to present to the gods at Cahuachi.

Sakai believes that up until 200 CE the Nazca walked these ritual pathways. His research team believes that from 200 CE to 450 CE, the lines were used for local religious rituals. Broken ceramic jars found at certain places along the Nazca Lines appear to have been used in some kind of religious ritual. However, by 450 CE Cahuachi was no longer used as a religious center. The Japanese research does not yet explain many things about the Nazca Lines. The team hopes to answer more questions as they continue their studies.

Are the Nazca Lines water maps, ritual pathways, or something else entirely? Perhaps they had many purposes. The mystery of the Nazca Lines will never be completely solved. The only people who know the meaning behind the geoglyphs have been gone for thousands of years.

PERSPECTIVES
Greenpeace: Heroes or Foes?

In December 2014, members of Greenpeace, an environmental group, went to the Nazca Lines site to lay down huge yellow letters on the desert floor. The message, TIME FOR CHANGE! THE FUTURE IS RENEWABLE, was aimed at a United Nations conference on climate change taking place in Lima, Peru, at that time. Peru's government was angry and demanded apologies, which it received from Greenpeace. Entrance into the area where the message had been placed is strictly prohibited without a permit. Special footwear is required to avoid damaging the fragile rocks. A footprint near or on a line might stay there for thousands of years.

Professor Masato Sakai speaks in Japan on new discoveries his team has made while working in Peru.

However, it is likely that researchers will continue to search for answers. Drawn to the mysterious past, people will continue their quest to understand the Nazca, who lived in this world long before we did.

EXPLORE ONLINE

Chapter Five gives some background about the work being done by Yamagata University in Japan. The article at the website below gives more information about these researchers' work. How is the information from the website the same as the information in Chapter Five? What new information did you learn from the website?

Pilgrimage Route
mycorelibrary.com/nazca-lines

WEIGHING THE EVIDENCE

The Nazca Lines are an astronomical calendar.

Evidence for:
- The lines and figures seem to point to certain stars and constellations.

Evidence against:
- Hawkins's computer study showed no connection between lines and stars other than what is expected by chance.

The Nazca Lines were built to be seen from balloons.

Evidence for:
- The lines and figures look clearest from the air.

Evidence against:
- The balloons that Jim Woodman built with local materials used reeds that were not available in the desert at the time the lines were constructed.

The Nazca Lines were a water map.

Evidence for:
- Some of the geometric figures mark where geological faults cross each other and where water can be found.
- Zigzag lines mark areas where there is no water.

Evidence against:
- The lines and figures are dense and cross each other in hundreds of places. It is not easy to sort out which figures and lines indicate water.

STOP AND THINK

Tell the Tale
Chapter One of this book discusses the first explorers to find the Nazca Lines. Imagine you are also exploring the deserts in Peru. Write 200 words describing your flight to the desert and what you saw from the airplane. Include a description of one of the figures you saw.

Another View
Most theories in this book indicate the Nazca Lines were completed by 600 CE. As you know, every source is different. Ask a librarian or another adult to help you find a source about the Nazca Lines. Write a short essay comparing and contrasting the new source's point of view with that of this book's author. What is the point of view of each author? How are they similar and why? How are they different and why?

You Are There

Imagine you are invited to investigate the Nazca Lines. Write a letter to your friends at home telling them what you have found. Describe some of the lines and figures. Which theory about the lines does your research support? Be sure to add plenty of detail.

Why Do I Care?

Maybe you have never seen the Nazca Lines in person. That does not mean you cannot think of ways to protect the lines. How does archaeology affect your life? Do you know anyone who studies ancient artifacts? How might learning more about the Nazca Lines impact the modern world?

GLOSSARY

aerial
taken from or seen from high above

archaeologist
a scientist that studies bones and tools of ancient people to learn about their lives and activities

faults
fractures in Earth's crust that have rock masses on each side of the break

fertilizer
a substance that is added to soil and helps plants grow

hemisphere
a half of Earth

manganese
a hard, pale gray metal that easily breaks

rituals
actions that are done as part of a ceremony that is often religious

shamans
people who are believed to use magic to cure people or control events

trapezoids
four-sided planes or figures having two parallel and two nonparallel sides

LEARN MORE

Books

Compoint, Stéphane. *Buried Treasures: Uncovering Secrets of the Past.* New York: Abrams Books for Young Readers, 2011.

The Mysteries in the Nazca Desert. Chicago: World Book, 2015.

Websites

To learn more about Mysteries of History, visit **booklinks.abdopublishing.com**. These links are routinely monitored and updated to provide the most current information available.

Visit **mycorelibrary.com** for free additional tools for teachers and students.

INDEX

aerial photographs, 15, 17, 20
Andes Mountains, 6–7
Aveni, Anthony, 14, 21

Bast, Robert, 30

Cahuachi, 5, 20, 38
Castro, Rossel, 28

desert varnish, 8, 9

El Niño, 30

Hawkins, Gerald, 19–21
hot-air balloons, 22–23

Johnson, David, 36

Kosok, Paul, 12–14, 16, 23

Mejia Xesspe, Toribio, 5, 9, 12, 36
Munck, Carl, 29
Mystery on the Desert, 16, 17

Nazca, 6–9, 14–15, 22–23, 27–28, 30, 35, 36–37, 38, 41

pottery, 7, 8
puquios, 37

Reiche, Maria, 11–16, 17

Silverman, Helaine, 8, 23
Stierlin, Henri, 28–29

theories,
 airfields, 22, 25
 astronomical calendar, 13–14, 16, 20–21, 23
 fabric workshop, 28
 farmland, 28
 flood memorial, 32
 ritual pathways, 36–39
 running tracks, 29–30
 sun worship, 22–23
 water map, 36, 39
von Breunig, George, 29–30
von Däniken, Erich, 22, 25

Woodman, Jim, 22–24

Yamagata University, 37, 41

ABOUT THE AUTHOR

Bonnie Hinman has more than 40 nonfiction children's books published. Hinman loves a good mystery, and the Nazca Lines mystery is one of the best. She lives in Joplin, Missouri, with her husband, and near her children and grandchildren.

H. 6/16